THE STORY OF ABU SIMBEL

**With the Highlights
of the History and Civilization
of Ancient Egypt**

Latif Doss
and Asham Besada

LONGMAN

LONGMAN GROUP LIMITED
Longman House
Burnt Mill, Harlow, Essex.

© Longman Group Ltd 1973

First published 1973
Third impression 1981

ISBN 0 582 76116 6
Set in Monophoto Baskerville

Printed in Hong Kong by
Wing Tai Cheung Printing Co Ltd

Contents

Acknowledgements

The authors wish to express their great thanks to the Egyptologists at the Centre of Documentation and Studies on Ancient Egypt, Cairo, for their valuable help.

We are also most grateful to them for permission to reproduce photographs for pages 9, 72 and 82, and to the following for permission to reproduce photographs. Middle East Archive (Alistair Duncan) for pages 2, 4, 7, 19, 25 and 31. UNESCO for pages 43, 45, 54, 62, 69, 72, 73, 75, 77, 79 and 81. Egyptian Tourist Office for pages 49 and 57. Picturepoint for page 40–1.

Introduction

Some years ago the whole world was talking about Abu Simbel. It was in great danger, and it had to be saved.

In this book you will be told the story of Abu Simbel. But you will first be made familiar with the story of Ancient Egypt. This is because the two stories are closely connected.

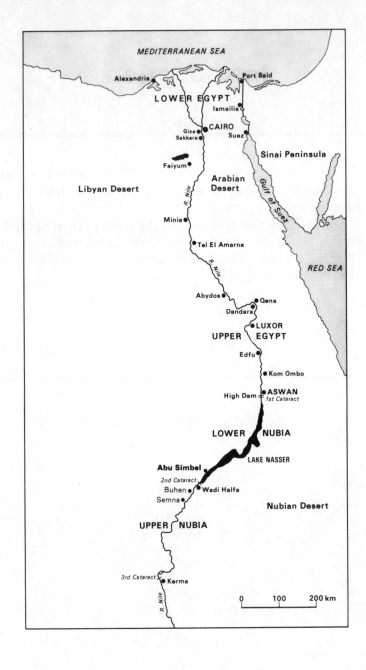

Chapter 1
The Builders of the Pyramids

Thousands of years ago a very civilized people lived in the Nile valley. Most of the people of the world were still trying to find their way in the dark. But the people in the Nile valley had developed a great civilization. They dug canals and cultivated the land. They built houses and palaces. They built splendid temples for their gods and immense tombs for their dead kings. We now call these wonderful people the Ancient Egyptians.

The Ancient Egyptians built their houses with bricks of mud. But they built the tombs of their kings with stone. At first the tomb was a heap of sand. It was covered and surrounded by blocks of stone. A block is a large piece of material which is used for building. The dead body of the king was placed in a little room which was under the ground. Then this simple tomb developed into a step-pyramid. This was a number of buildings placed one on top of the other. There is a step-pyramid at

The Step-Pyramid of King Zoser at Sakkara

The Builders of the Pyramids

Sakkara near Cairo. This step-pyramid was built for King Zoser by Imhoteb, who was the King's minister and architect. An architect is a man who helps to make buildings. He draws plans and looks after the work. Imhoteb was also a great doctor and wise man. Many years after his death he became a god of medicine.

The step-pyramid was improved until it became a pyramid. The architects made rapid progress in the art of building. The Ancient Egyptians built many pyramids. But the most wonderful of these is the *Great Pyramid of Giza* near Cairo.

The Great Pyramid was built for King Khufu, who ruled over Egypt five thousand years ago. "The kings who came before me," said Khufu, "built for themselves great tombs of solid rock. But I will build a tomb that shall live until the end of time."

There was much truth in the King's words. His great tomb has lived for thousands of years. It still stands high at the edge of the desert and covers a large piece of ground. It is one hundred and thirty-six metres high, and covers about fifty-three thousand square metres of ground.

Two million, three hundred thousand blocks of stone were used for building that great tomb. Each block weighed about two and a half tons. The blocks were cut from the hills across the river. Then they were put on big ships and taken down the Nile. But how were these heavy blocks dragged to the position of the Pyramid? A big road was made from the bank of the river to the desert. The blocks were dragged along this road.

To build the Pyramid, the King employed architects. He also employed a great number of workmen. It was said that one hundred thousand men were employed. For twenty years they continued to work on that great

The Pyramids of Giza

royal tomb. But they worked only during the Nile flood. During that time they had no work in the fields.

The opening of the Pyramid was on the north side. It was closed by an immense stone. The builders were so clever that the stone could not be easily recognized. It looked exactly like the other stones on the surface of the Pyramid. The opening led to a long narrow passage. Another passage led to the room in which the King was buried.

Near the Great Pyramid, there are two other pyramids. They are like the Great Pyramid, but they are much smaller. There are many other pyramids in the desert. Each pyramid was a royal tomb.

Why did the Ancient Egyptians build such strong and immense tombs? They did so because they believed in a life after death. They believed that one day the dead person would return to life. They thought that the soul would come back to the dead body. It was therefore necessary to keep the body in a safe place. It was also necessary to preserve the body. So they embalmed the dead bodies of their kings. An embalmed body does not decay and it is called a mummy. You can still see the mummies of the kings of Ancient Egypt in the museum in Cairo. A museum is a building where old and interesting objects are kept. For thousands of years the dead bodies of these ancient kings have been preserved. Indeed, the Ancient Egyptians were very clever at the art of embalming.

It was also the custom of the Ancient Egyptians to put the king's treasures in the royal tomb. But there were tomb-robbers who might come and steal the treasures. They might damage the mummy. If the mummy were damaged or destroyed, the dead person could not return to life. So the Ancient Egyptians made statues which looked like the kings. Many statues were put in the tombs. So, if the mummy were damaged or destroyed, the soul of the dead king would go to the statue. The dead king would therefore be able to return to life. The Ancient Egyptians made fine statues. They made them usually of stone, but sometimes of gold and precious stones.

A very strange statue which they made lies near the Great Pyramid. This is the *Sphinx*. It is an immense figure cut out in the solid rock. It looks like a lion with its paws stretched out. But it has a human head and face. The face has been much damaged, but it still has a mysterious look. For thousands of years it has looked upon the wide desert and the green valley. People who see this statue wonder at the mysterious look on its face. Some admire it; others fear it. The Arabic name of the Sphinx is "Abu Elhaul" which means "the Father of Fear".

The Ancient Egyptians put statues in their temples, where they worshipped their gods. The Ancient Egyptians worshipped many gods, but the greatest of them was the sun-god, *Ra*. Every morning he appeared in the east, and began his daily journey. On his way he looked down upon his people. He saw their good deeds and evil deeds. He gave them light and heat. In the evening he passed beyond the mountain in the west. Then he went down into the underworld. The underworld is the place of the dead.

The Ancient Egyptians also worshipped *Isis* and *Osiris*. They believed in an interesting story about them. They thought that Isis and Osiris at first appeared on earth. Osiris was a tall and strong young man. Isis was a very beautiful woman. She was the sister of Osiris and she was also his wife. It was the custom of important men in Ancient Egypt to marry their sisters and daughters.

Isis and Osiris lived among the people and helped them. Isis looked after the sick children and cured many

6

The Sphinx

of them. Osiris helped the farmers in the fields. In the evening he used to sit with them and play music to them. The people liked Isis and Osiris very much. They liked Osiris so much that they made him king. They also made Isis queen.

One day an evil-looking man came to the King's palace. He asked to see the King. He said that he was the King's brother. The man's name was Set. There was a band of men with him who were carrying weapons.

The King welcomed Set and invited him to stay in the palace. But Set was a wicked and cruel man. He wanted to become king himself. So he planned to kill the King. He prepared a splendid feast and invited the King. When the meal had ended, he ordered his men to bring a big box. The box was so big that a man could lie inside it. But it was a beautiful box. "I will give the box to any man," said Set. "But it must fit him perfectly."

One man after another climbed into the box, but it was too big for anyone. "O King, will you not try?" cried Set. "It would be a suitable box for the royal clothes." Osiris hesitated at first. But at last he rose and walked towards the box. He climbed into it. It fitted him perfectly. Then he tried to get out. But Set was too quick for him. With a shout he rushed to the box and closed the heavy lid. Then he ordered his men to throw the box into the river.

Isis heard of the death of her husband. She learnt how he was cruelly murdered. She felt very sad. But she decided to look for the box which contained her husband's body. She searched for the box in many places. She travelled to distant lands. At last she found the box.

Isis was a goddess. She had great power. She managed to bring her dead husband back to life. For two years Isis and Osiris had a happy life. Then Set discovered the place where they lived. One day he followed Osiris and

The Goddess Isis

killed him. He cut his body into fourteen pieces. He buried each piece in a different part of the country.

Isis was overcome by sorrow, but she did not lose hope. She was confident of her power. She travelled far and suffered much. But she was determined to find the pieces, however much she suffered. At last she succeeded in collecting all the pieces. She put them together, and again she was able to bring her dead husband back to life.

But Osiris did not stay long on earth. "The gods have decided," he said to his wife, "that I should join them now." And so he went away. He became king and judge of the underworld. He was the chief god of the underworld.

* * *

During the time of the first pyramids, the king of Egypt was a strong and powerful ruler. He was very greatly respected by the people. They believed that he was almost a god. They respected him so much that they did not mention him by name. Instead, they spoke of the palace in which he lived. They called it the "Great House" or *Pharaoh*. That was why the kings of Ancient Egypt were called Pharaohs.

The Pharaoh lived in a splendid palace which had two gates. One gate pointed to Upper Egypt and the other to Lower Egypt. Before the rule of the Pharaohs, Upper and Lower Egypt had been two separate kingdoms. Each kingdom had a different crown. The crown of Upper Egypt was white in colour and that of Lower Egypt was red. Then the two kingdoms were united into one. The two crowns were also put together and made into one crown. We call it a "double crown", because it has two parts.

The Builders of the Pyramids

The king was surrounded by princes, nobles, ministers and architects. The princes were the sons of the king. The nobles and the ministers helped the king to govern the country. The architects helped him to build the pyramid and the temples. Sometimes the chief minister was the eldest son of the king. He would therefore gain much experience in government before becoming a king.

Ancient Egypt was divided into several districts, and there was a local ruler for each district. The ruler managed the affairs of his district. He commanded the local army. He collected taxes. There were no coins in those days. People exchanged one article for another. A pot was exchanged for a fish; a bundle of wheat for a fan; a wooden box for a goat. The taxes therefore were cattle, sheep, chickens, crops and manufactured articles. A number of clerks helped the local ruler.

The clerk was an important person. Rich people employed clerks. There were also clerks in the Government and in the temples. Good clerks were chosen by the king to have important positions in the Government.

A child who was going to be a clerk was sent to school. At school he learnt how to read and write. He learnt *Hieroglyphic*, which was the Ancient Egyptian writing. Hieroglyphic means "sacred writing". At first the letters of that ancient language were pictures. There were pictures of animals, of birds, and of objects. After that there was a development in the system of writing. The pictures developed into signs. Writers could therefore write more easily and more quickly.

The Ancient Egyptians wrote on stone and on wood. They wrote on the walls of tombs and on the walls of temples. But for a long time the Ancient Egyptian writing was a puzzle for the modern world. No one was able to understand what the signs meant. Then, towards the end of the eighteenth century, a stone was found near

Rosetta. This is a town in Lower Egypt, near the sea. It was not a big stone, but it was of great value. One side of the stone was covered with writing in three languages. There was the old Egyptian writing at the top. Under this there was the later Egyptian writing. At the bottom there was writing in Greek.

People believed that the Ancient Egyptian writing on the stone had been translated into Greek. Because Greek could be understood, so could the Ancient Egyptian writing. The *Rosetta Stone* was therefore an important discovery. All the Ancient Egyptian writings have, since then, been translated. We now know much of the history of the Ancient Egyptians.

The Ancient Egyptians did not write only on stone and wood. They also wrote on *papyrus*. Papyrus is a tall plant which grows in marshes. Marshes are low lands which are covered with water. Papyrus grew in the marshes of Lower Egypt. The Ancient Egyptians cut the papyrus into thin strips. Then they stuck the strips together and made them into sheets. When one sheet had been made, another was joined to the end of it. Sometimes the sheet of papyrus was many metres long. When all was finished, the papyrus was rolled up. Then it was tied with string and stored away.

The Ancient Egyptians were the first people in the world who used paper. Indeed, the word "paper" comes from "papyrus".

Other articles were also made of papyrus. The Ancient Egyptians made shoes, ropes, mats and baskets of papyrus. They also made boats by tying together bundles of papyrus with ropes. But not all their boats were made of papyrus. They also made boats of wood in which they sailed along the Nile. The boats carried crops and other articles from one place to another. The Ancient Egyptians also crossed the seas and traded

with other countries. They sailed across the Mediter-
ranean and traded with many countries on its coast.
They sailed through the Red Sea and reached Punt in
East Africa. Punt is now called Somalia.

In 1970 a brave sailor named Thor Heyerdahl made a
large boat of papyrus. He called his papyrus boat *Ra* and
he sailed in it across the Atlantic Ocean. He managed
to reach the coast of America. He proved that a papyrus
boat could cross the ocean. But did the Ancient Egyptians reach the coast of America in their boats? Did they
carry their civilization to the ancient people who lived
there? We don't yet know.

Papyrus was not cultivated. It grew as a wild plant
in the marshes of Ancient Egypt. So did the lotus. The
lotus is another plant which grows in water. But other
plants were cultivated by the Ancient Egyptians.
Indeed, Ancient Egypt was the first great agricultural
country in the world. And a great part of the wealth of
the country depended on agriculture. Each year the
great river covered the fields with water. Then, when
the water went down, the farmers cultivated the land.
They used an axe to dig the earth, and they also used a
wooden plough. They were the first people in the world
to use the axe and the plough. They grew various kinds
of crops, but their chief crop was wheat. During the
harvest they gathered the crops and carried them to
store-houses. On a big farm a clerk was employed to
watch the work. He counted the bags of crops in the
store-houses and wrote down the number.

One of the crops which the Ancient Egyptians grew
was flax. They cultivated it and then made it into cloth.
They spun the flax into threads and wove the threads
into fine linen. The linen was as fine as the best silk
material which is produced at present. Men and
women in Ancient Egypt wore simple clothes made of

linen. Most men wore short clothes that covered the lower part of the body. Men's clothes hardly reached the knee.

Women were dressed in thin tight clothes. A woman's dress was long, but did not cover the arms. Rich ladies were fond of jewels. A rich lady wore a necklace round her neck and a bracelet round her arm. She also put false hair on her head. Indeed, some of the ladies' fashionable dresses today are not very different from the dresses worn by Egyptian ladies thousands of years ago.

These fine linen clothes and these beautiful jewels show that the Ancient Egyptians were clever workmen. They made jewellery of gold and precious stones. They made boxes, chairs, beds and other pieces of furniture of wood. They also made pots and bowls of glass and clay, and tools and weapons of iron and copper. The museums of the world are full of the fine articles which the Ancient Egyptian workmen made.

The Ancient Egyptians were also clever artists. Their stone and gold statues and their pictures on the walls of tombs and temples show their skill in art. They loved beauty. The palace of the king and the houses of the rich were full of beautiful objects and ornaments. The roofs and walls of the rooms were covered with pictures of animals, birds and flowers. Even the floor was covered with beautiful scenes of marshes, water and fish.

Besides art, they were fond of music. Their musical instruments were the harp and the flute. At the royal palace and at the houses of the rich, parties were given. Men played the flute. Women sang, danced and played the harp and the sistrum. The sistrum is an instrument which is shaken. The Ancient Egyptians were gay people. They liked to enjoy life.

* * *

One of the great Pharaohs who ruled over Egypt after King Khufu was *Amenemhet the Third*. He became king about four thousand years ago. During his time, Egypt enjoyed peace and became a very rich country.

Amenemhet thought of a plan to increase the wealth of the country. There is a great oasis in the desert west of the Nile. We now call this low land, which has water and trees, Fayum. Amenemhet changed this oasis into a great reservoir. A reservoir is a large artificial lake. When the Nile was in flood, much water was stored in this reservoir. It was called Lake Moeris. When the water of the Nile fell, water was let out of the reservoir. This water was used for cultivating the fields.

Until the time of Amenemhet, the capital of Egypt had been Memphis, near Sakkara. But Amenemhet did not live at Memphis. He built a splendid palace near Lake Moeris. This was the royal palace. It was also the centre of government for the whole country. It contained twelve halls and three thousand rooms. Every year the local rulers came to this palace with their men. Each ruler went to the rooms which were given to him. Together with his men he discussed the taxes which they had to pay to the Government. The palace was also an important religious building. The local rulers and their men worshipped their gods in the halls of the palace.

It is unfortunate that no traces of this wonderful palace remain. But in the past many travellers saw it and greatly admired it. They called it the Labyrinth. Labyrinth means a complicated system of winding paths. For it was difficult for the visitor to find his way through the rooms and paths of this great palace.

Chapter 2
The Builders of the Temples

Amenemhet was a powerful ruler and a great king. But after Amenemhet not all the Pharaohs were as powerful as he had been. Weak Pharaohs ruled over Egypt. Local rulers grew in strength. The weaker the Pharaohs grew, the stronger the local rulers became. The local rulers gradually gained independence. They quarrelled with each other, and they struggled to become Pharaohs.

Foreign people took advantage of the unhappy condition of the nation, and attacked Lower Egypt. These foreign people were the *Hyksos*, who came from Asia. For more than a century the Hyksos ruled over Egypt. They set up their capital at Avaris in Lower Egypt. They were not as civilized as the Egyptians. They burnt many Egyptian cities and destroyed many Egyptian temples.

The Hyksos were also cruel people. They treated the Egyptians badly. There is a story about one of their kings in Avaris. He sent a message to the local ruler at

Thebes, which was an important town in Upper Egypt. The King told him that the noise of the hippopotami in the river was disturbing his sleep! Hippopotami are very large animals which live for most of the time in rivers. The King threatened to kill the hippopotami at Thebes. This annoyed the Egyptians. They considered that the hippopotamus was a sacred animal.

At last the local rulers of Egypt made war against the Hyksos. Ahmose, the local ruler of Thebes, led the fight against the Hyksos. His soldiers surrounded Avaris and conquered it. Then the Egyptians drove the Hyksos out of the country. They followed them into Asia and conquered many of their cities there.

But the war with the Hyksos was a useful experience for the Egyptians. They learnt much from this experience. They now had an organized army which was divided into groups. They learnt how to use the bow, the arrow and the axe. Indeed, their skill in using these weapons often frightened their enemies. The Hyksos also brought horses to Egypt. The horse had not been known to the Egyptians before. Horses were used for pulling chariots. The Egyptians learnt how to use chariots in war.

Now Thebes became the capital of Egypt. Amon, the sun-god of Thebes, became the most important god in the country. The temples grew into splendid palaces, and the High Priest of Amon was now a powerful person. He had great political power.

But although Amon was now the chief god, Osiris was still worshipped. Osiris was the great judge and king in the underworld. Every good man might return from the dead as Osiris had done. Every dead man would stand before Osiris and forty-two judges. His heart would be weighed against a feather, which represented goodness and truth. This was to decide whether the dead man was a good person. A good person would go to the fields of peace. Evil persons would be attacked by a wild beast. They would be thrown into a deep hole.

To help the dead person in the underworld, a roll of papyrus was put in his tomb. The roll contained prayers and magic writings. We now call this roll of papyrus the *Book of the Dead*.

* * *

Years passed after the death of brave King Ahmose who drove the Hyksos out of the country. Then a woman became Pharaoh. The woman was *Queen Hatshepsut*. She was a beautiful and clever woman. She was the first great woman in history.

At first, Hatshepsut ruled with her husband, King Thutmose the Third. But she was an ambitious woman. She wanted to have all the power in her hands. The priests of Amon agreed with her. They declared that the gods had chosen her to rule alone over Egypt. The priests were very powerful. So for many years Hatshepsut ruled alone.

The first thing that the Queen did was to continue building her temple at Thebes. She had already started building this temple on the west bank of the Nile. It was built at the side of the cliff. The temple is different from the other great temples of those days. It has three terraces, one terrace on top of the other. A terrace is a raised space which is made in the side of a hill or a cliff. Hatshepsut's temple is now called the temple of Dir-el-Bahri.

Hatshepsut built the temple in honour of the god Amon. She decided to plant myrrh-trees from Punt, on the terraces. So she prepared five ships. The ships sailed

The Temple of Hatshepsut at Dir-el-Bahri

down the Nile and reached the Red Sea. They used an ancient canal which connected the east branch of the Nile with the Red Sea.

The ships were loaded with various goods from Egypt. One ship carried a statue of Queen Hatshepsut, and this statue was erected in Punt. Besides myrrh-trees, the ships brought back gold and incense. Incense is a substance of great value. It produces a sweet smell and smoke, when it is burned.

The ships returned to Egypt. They sailed up the Nile and reached Thebes. Besides the trees, the gold and the incense, there were a number of natives and animals in the ships. The people of Thebes saw the natives, the animals and the goods of that distant land. They wondered at what they saw. You can still see the beautiful pictures of this wonderful voyage. They can be seen on the walls of the Queen's temple at Dir-el-Bahri.

Hatshepsut also erected two great obelisks. An obelisk is a high stone post with four sides. It is pointed at the top. Hatshepsut erected the obelisks for the god Amon and in memory of her father. She erected the obelisks in the temple of Karnak. This temple at Thebes had been built by several kings. The obelisks rose high in the temple and were covered with gold and silver. Each obelisk was thirty metres high and weighed about three hundred and fifty tons. "They shall be seen from great distances," said Hatshepsut, "and they shall fill the land with their light."

One of these obelisks still stands at the temple of Karnak. It is greatly admired by the visitors who come to Thebes.

When Hatshepsut died, *Thutmose the Third* ruled over Egypt. He hated the memory of Hatshepsut, who had refused to let him rule with her. So he covered the sides of her obelisks with plaster. But as years passed, the plaster fell off. The Queen's name and deeds can still be seen on her obelisk at Karnak. They show the modern world how great she was.

* * *

For many years the people in Asia had not seen an Egyptian army. This encouraged them to rebel against Egypt. The King of Kadesh was the Pharaoh's worst enemy. He was the King of the Hittites. These were an ancient people who lived in Asia at that time. The King of Kadesh urged other cities to rebel against Egypt. So King Thutmose the Third marched into Asia and attacked his enemies. The King himself, in his beautiful chariot, led the attack. Thutmose was a brave soldier and a great general. The battle did not last long. The enemy was defeated and the enemy soldiers ran away. The camp of the King of Kadesh was taken by the Egyptians. The Egyptians also took hundreds of horses and chariots and great quantities of gold and silver. They had won a great victory over their enemies. King Thutmose appointed new rulers in Asia and then returned to Egypt.

At Thebes the King started to add new buildings to the Karnak temple. He built halls with beautiful rows of columns. A column is a tall upright post. He also offered to the god Amon many of the treasures which he had brought from Asia. Indeed, Amon's fortune was immense.

Thutmose also erected a number of obelisks. But not all these obelisks are now in Egypt. They were carried to other countries. They now stand high in the public squares of many foreign countries. They remind the world of the skill and art of the Ancient Egyptians.

Thutmose the Third fought many battles in Asia and

in the south of Egypt. He conquered many lands. These conquests brought Egypt much wealth. The more conquests he made, the richer his country became.

Thebes was now a great city with splendid temples and fine houses. In later times people wondered at its great temples. Perhaps this was why they called it Luxor. Luxor means "the City of Palaces". It is the name of the present town which is near the temple of Karnak. The fine houses and the splendid palaces of Thebes have disappeared. But the wonderful temples still remain.

During the time of Thutmose the Third, the name of the Pharaoh was feared and respected everywhere. For many years after his death, Egypt continued to make progress. Then a weak ruler became king. This was Amenhotep the Fourth. Amenhotep was greatly interested in religion. Indeed, he loved religion more than anything else.

Amenhotep did not like the worship of many gods. He believed in one god only. He wanted the people to worship one god only. He wanted them to worship the sun-god, whom he called *Aton*. To make them forget the old gods, he closed the temples. He also sent away the priests. His own name, Amenhotep, meant "Amon rests". So he changed it to *Ikhnaton*, which meant "Aton is satisfied".

Thebes reminded the King of the god Amon, whom he particularly hated. So he left Thebes and built a new city farther down the Nile. He called the new city Akhetaton, which means "the Heaven of Aton". It is called in modern times Tel-el-Amarna.

At Akhetaton he built a temple for the god Aton. He often went to the temple to offer sacrifices to Aton. His beautiful wife, Queen Nefertiti, usually went with him. The beautiful Queen and her four pretty daughters attended the ceremonies at the temple.

Ikhnaton was also a poet. He wrote beautiful songs in honour of the god Aton. The following lines show the beauty of the King's faith in Aton:

> *Bright is the earth*
> *When you rise in the heaven,*
> *When you shine as Aton by day.*
> *The darkness disappears*
> *When you send out your light;*
> *The Two Lands are in daily feast,*
> *Awake and standing upon their feet.*
>
> *The birds fly in the marshes,*
> *Their wings uplifted in your praise.*
> *All the sheep dance upon their feet,*
> *All winged things fly,*
> *They live when you have shone upon them.*
>
> *You are in my heart,*
> *There is no other that knows you,*
> *Except your son Ikhnaton.*

Ikhnaton saw his god as a kind father, who looked after all men and all creatures. Even the birds in the marshes lifted up their wings to praise him.

But a new faith like this could hardly be understood by the common people in those days. The priests of Amon were annoyed. They made plans against Ikhnaton. So there was trouble in Egypt. There was also trouble in the conquered countries in Asia. The most powerful enemies of the Egyptians in Asia were the Hittites.

Rulers who were still loyal to the Pharaoh sent messages to him. They told him that the situation was serious and they asked him for help. They even sent their brothers and their sons to the Pharaoh to ask him for help. But they did not get any reply. Sometimes a very small army was sent. But such a small army could hardly make the situation better.

Ikhnaton had probably never been strong. His troubles also had a bad effect on his health. At last he died. He was buried in a tomb which his servants had dug for him. The tomb was in a lonely valley which was some miles to the east of his city.

Ikhnaton was followed, after a short time, by Tuten-khaton. Tutenkhaton means "the Living Picture of Aton". The priests of Amon made him leave Akhetaton and live at Thebes. At Thebes he continued to worship Aton. But soon the priests made him worship Amon. They also made him change his name to *Tutenkhamon*, which means "the Living Picture of Amon".

Tutenkhamon did not rule for a long time. When he died, he was buried in a tomb in the *Valley of the Kings*. This valley lies on the west bank of the Nile. It is opposite the temple of Karnak. The Pharaohs had now stopped building pyramids. Such big tombs as the pyramids often attracted robbers. The treasures which were buried with the kings were discovered and stolen by robbers. For this reason the Pharaohs now preferred to be buried in the Valley of the Kings.

For six hundred years the Pharaohs were buried on the west bank of the Nile. Their tombs were dug deep into the side of the hill. There were secret doors and hidden passages to deceive the robbers. The openings of the tombs were closed with care and were hidden out of sight. But, in spite of this, tomb-robbers found their way to the tombs. They stole the treasures which they contained.

But the treasures of the tomb of Tutenkhamon were not stolen. For more than three thousand years the treasures of the young Pharaoh escaped discovery. There

The gold coffin of Tutenkhamon

were thousands of articles in the tomb. The Ancient Egyptians believed that the King would need these articles in the underworld. There were golden thrones, royal seats, chariots of war, fine statues and boxes full of jewels. All these treasures are now kept in the museum in Cairo.

The mummy of the King was put in a coffin of solid gold. This gold coffin was kept inside a wooden coffin with a gold surface. The two coffins were put in a third coffin which was made of wood and covered with gold. All these coffins were placed inside four big wooden boxes. The boxes were covered with gold and were placed one inside the other.

This shows us how rich the Pharaohs were. But Tutenkhamon was not a great Pharaoh. Nor did he rule for a long time. So treasures of greater value might have been buried with more famous Pharaohs. But it is unfortunate that such treasures were taken away by tomb-robbers.

In the side of the hill near the tomb of Tutenkhamon, there is another tomb. This is the tomb of *King Seti the First*. King Seti's tomb is one of the largest and most splendid tombs discovered in the Valley of the Kings. It goes down into the mountain about one hundred and twenty metres. It contains several passages and large halls with columns. The columns, the walls and the roof are covered with writings and paintings. After thousands of years these wonderful paintings still preserve their bright colours.

Seti the First was a powerful king. He organized an army and made plans to get back the lost lands in Asia. He fought against his enemies, the Hittites, and defeated them. But he was unable to conquer Kadesh, their strong city.

In Egypt, King Seti started to repair the temples.

They had been badly damaged during the time of Ikhnaton. Seti also built a temple at Abydos. And at Karnak he erected a great part of the hall of columns.

King Seti knew that his son Ramses would be king after him. So he realized that his education was very important. The prince was trained in sports and in the art of war. His education also included history, religion and politics. It was important that he should be able to carry out the various duties of a king.

When Seti felt that his death was near, he made a decision. He decided to let Ramses rule with him. "Put the crown on his head," Seti said to the nobles of the court, "so that I may see his power. I want to see his power while I am alive."

At last Seti died and his body was embalmed. When the day of the funeral came, the new King, *Ramses the Second*, led the procession. The procession crossed the Nile at Thebes and reached the tomb in the Valley of the Kings. The coffin was put down into the tomb and the dead Pharaoh was left in his last resting-place.

But King Ramses the Second felt that he had not done enough for such a kind father. So, in his royal ship, he sailed down the Nile to Abydos. At Abydos he went to the temple of his father and offered sacrifices to the gods. Then he made a long speech to his father.

"See, you have entered heaven," said Ramses. "You are now with Ra, among the stars and the moon. When Ra rises in the heaven, your eyes are fixed on his beauty. I have looked after your temple every day. My heart surrounds you with love and sympathy. I will keep the memory of your name while you are in the underworld. All shall go well for you as long as I live."

Ramses believed that King Seti, in the underworld, understood every word of his speech. He imagined that King Seti answered him. "Rejoice greatly, dear son," said Seti. "I have asked Ra to give you many years on earth. I have also asked Osiris to do the same. All the gods shall take care of you."

Ramses had now done his duty. He had shown respect to a loving father, both in Thebes and at Abydos. There was no reason now to make him stay in the south. Once more he sailed in his royal ship towards the north. He had chosen a city in Lower Egypt to be his capital. He did not want to stay at Thebes. He wanted to avoid the heat of the summer in the south.

But there was a stronger reason that persuaded him to go. Ramses had received alarming news from Asia. The Hittites were again making trouble. Ramses decided to punish them. So he collected a strong army and divided it into four groups. Each group was given the name of one of the great gods: Amon, Ra, Ptah and Set. Ramses himself led the group which was given the name of Amon. Then he marched with his group towards Kadesh.

The enemy sent two men to Ramses to deceive him. They told him that the Hittite king had gone to the north. So, without waiting for the rest of his army, Ramses advanced towards the city of Kadesh. He reached the city and set up his camp there.

Ramses almost fell into the trap which had been made for him. He found himself surrounded by enemy soldiers. They had been hiding out of sight. The two Hittites had deceived him. So they were brought before him and were given a thorough beating. They confessed the truth. They had been trying to get secret information about the Egyptian army. They also confessed that they had lied. Their king had not gone to the north.

King Ramses was now in a dangerous situation. But he did not hesitate for a moment. The brave Pharaoh decided to fight. He seized his weapons and got into his chariot. He prayed to Amon to help him, and then rushed at his enemies. Enemy soldiers fell before him or ran away in great fear. Ramses rushed at the enemy again and again. At last the rest of his army arrived, and the enemy was defeated. The Hittite king ran away.

After this great victory, Ramses returned to Egypt. But soon he had to go back to Asia. The Hittites had again rebelled against him. For fifteen years, Ramses made war against the Hittites. At last their king died. The new king preferred peace to war. He preferred to make peace with the Pharaoh.

"What has happened?" he said to his men. "Our country is in a sad condition. Our master is angry with us. Heaven no longer gives us water. Let us give the Pharaoh our best possessions. I will offer him my own daughter. We will take our presents and go to Egypt. Then the great Pharaoh will give us peace and we will live."

And so the Hittite king and his daughter travelled to Egypt. They took with them presents of great value. They took horses, oxen, goats, sheep and much gold and silver.

King Ramses learnt of their coming. He rejoiced. He sent his men to meet them. At last the princess and her father arrived. The princess was very beautiful. Ramses married the lovely princess and gave her an Egyptian name. He called her Manefrure, which means "she who sees the beauty of Ra".

But the Hittite princess was not the King's only wife. He had several other wives and more than one hundred and fifty children.

Ramses built many temples. On the walls of these temples he wrote the stories of his wars. At Abu Simbel in Nubia he built two great temples. At Thebes he built a funeral temple on the west bank. It is now known as the *Ramesseum*. He also completed the splendid hall of columns at Karnak. This great hall contains one hundred and thirty-four big columns. Twelve of these columns are very thick. Six men with stretched arms can hardly surround one column.

Ramses was also fond of erecting statues and obelisks. Many of these obelisks are at present in foreign countries. One great statue of the King now stands in the middle of an important public square in Cairo.

King Ramses the Second ruled over Egypt for sixty-seven years. He was over ninety years old when he died. He was buried in the Valley of the Kings. But his reputation still lives and his great deeds are still remembered. Indeed, he deserves to be called "Ramses the Great".

The head of Ramses II at the Luxor Temple

Chapter 3
Nubia

King Ramses the Second built many temples in Nubia. But the most wonderful of these are the two temples at Abu Simbel. The temples will be described later. But let us first make ourselves familiar with the ancient history of Nubia.

For thousands of years this ancient land has been one of the most important parts of Africa. Compared with other parts of the Nile valley, it is almost a desert. But many important events happened on its soil. These events have had a great effect on the development of civilization. For some of the most important battles in ancient history were fought in Nubia. There was a long struggle between the people of the north and the people of the south.

The Ancient Egyptians were moving to the south. They wanted the gold of Nubia. They wanted to obtain gold from the gold-mines in the south. They called gold "nub" and they believed that Nubia was the land of gold. At the same time, the people in the south were moving to the north. They wanted to reach wider and richer parts of the Nile valley.

But where is Nubia? It is now divided between Egypt and the Sudan. The Nubian land now forms the south of Egypt and the north of the Sudan. But there are no exact boundaries for Nubia. The Ancient Egyptians often called it "Ta-kens". Ta-kens means "the Land of the Bend". But this was a general name. The Ancient Egyptians always distinguished between Lower Nubia and Upper Nubia. They called Lower Nubia, which was between the first and second cataracts, Wawat. They called Upper Nubia, which was south of the second cataract, Kush. Cataracts are the steep parts of a river where it flows quickly over rocks. There are many cataracts in the Nile.

In some ways the people of Wawat were like their neighbours in the south, the people of Kush. But they were two different races. The people of Wawat loved peace. The people of Kush were fond of war. Many of them became soldiers in the armies of the Pharaohs.

* * *

The Ancient Egyptians were greatly interested in Nubia. Their interest began long ago, in the age of the pyramids. Even before the time of King Khufu, the Egyptians went south, as far as the second cataract. They conquered Lower Nubia and brought back a large number of cattle.

Recent discoveries at Buhen show that the Egyptians settled in Lower Nubia. They settled there for more than two hundred and fifty years. They made great use of the natural wealth of the land. Copper was dug out and made into tools and weapons. Diorite was also discovered, and many royal statues were made from this beautiful stone.

Egyptian papyrus and Egyptian pots have been discovered at Buhen. The names of many of the first Pharaohs have been found on papyrus messages. Buhen was a town in the south which was important for trading. Donkeys loaded with ivory, incense and animal-skins passed through Buhen. They were sent to Egypt. Ivory is the white bone which is obtained from the teeth of elephants. It is of great value.

The strong rule of the Egyptians lasted a long time. Then came weak Pharaohs who could not control Nubia. Egypt lost her possessions in the south. A cattle-owning people came into Nubia. They settled between the first and second cataracts and lived on the banks of the river. They wore leather clothes and on their arms they wore bracelets of ivory and shell. Their houses were round huts of wood and grass. They buried their dead under heaps of earth. Their simple tombs were protected by circular stone walls. Rough clay models of cattle, sheep and goats have been found in these tombs.

Then strong rulers governed Egypt. People again became interested in the south. Once more the Egyptians managed to control Lower Nubia. Some years later, they started to build a number of fortresses. These fortresses protected Egyptian possessions against attacks. They also guarded roads which were important for trade.

The largest and finest of these fortresses was built at Buhen. This fortress enclosed many buildings. There were houses for common people and buildings for soldiers. A temple and a palace were also built. The palace was for the local ruler. Very thick and high brick walls surrounded and protected this small town. A wide and deep ditch was dug round the walls.

The strongest part of the fortress of Buhen was its great gate. It was built in the centre of the west wall. It was therefore opposite the long roads which passed across the desert. The gate was closed by double doors. Beyond the doors there was a wooden drawbridge. This was a bridge which could be raised in time of war. It would not be easy for any attacking enemy to enter the fortress. The enemy would be driven back by a rain of arrows from the soldiers defending the walls.

The building of fortresses must have cost the Egyptians much money and much effort. But this expense was necessary. The fortresses made it easy for the Egyptians to control Nubia. They went as far south as Semna and their power and influence went even farther.

The level of the Nile flood was measured at Semna. During the flood it was eight metres higher than it is now. More rain must therefore have fallen at that time. Otherwise the natives could not have kept such large numbers of cattle.

The Ancient Egyptians were interested in measuring the Nile flood. It was important to them. The measurements taken at Semna were reported to the Government in Egypt. The Government could therefore know the amount of crops which could be expected. For the higher the flood, the more crops could be expected. The Government could then decide what taxes farmers should pay.

* * *

Egyptian rule over Nubia lasted a long time. Then Egypt herself came under the rule of the Hyksos. Much of Egypt's power in Nubia was therefore lost. Egyptian fortresses were seized. Some were destroyed. The fortress of Buhen was set on fire.

But a large part of Lower Nubia was still controlled by the Egyptians. Many Egyptians had already settled in Lower Nubia. The cruel Hyksos had made them escape to the south and live there. Egyptian jewels, weapons, tools and other articles have been discovered in tombs in Lower Nubia.

At last the Hyksos' rule over Egypt came to an end. Brave King Ahmose drove them out of the country. Then he turned to the south. The second conquest of Nubia began.

It is not known how far south the Egyptians went. But there is no doubt that they reached the second cataract. They now possessed the whole of Nubia as far as the second cataract. They took possession of the ruins of the great fortress of Buhen. They started to rebuild it. A wide ditch was dug and towers were built. The surrounding walls were now of great strength. They were five metres thick and at least twelve metres high. Many other ruined fortresses were also rebuilt and made larger. For it was necessary to guard the important road to the gold-mines.

After King Ahmose had died, the conquest of Nubia continued. Then, at last, there was peace. The great conquering Pharaoh, Thutmose the Third, sent an army into the south. But he wished to show his power rather than to conquer the land. Almost the whole of Nubia was now a part of Egypt. Nubian gold, cattle and ivory were sent to Thebes.

* * *

When Seti became king, he was very interested in the gold-mines in Nubia. But the road to the gold-mines was in the heart of the desert. Men who were sent to get gold suffered much. They suffered because there was no water there. Seti's men dug a well, but no water came out.

King Ramses the Second was also interested in the Nubian gold-mines. He was particularly interested in the gold-mines of Akita, which is now called Wadi-el-Alaki. There was much gold at Akita, but there was no water. Men died of thirst on the road. So did their donkeys which they drove before them.

King Ramses therefore gave orders for another attempt to be made. His men attempted to find water. They succeeded. Water was found. After this, much gold could be obtained. The King was greatly delighted. He was more fortunate than his father.

* * *

Almost every Pharaoh erected a statue or built a temple in Nubia. Some of the temples can even be compared with the great temples of Luxor. Queen Hatshepsut built a temple inside the fortress of Buhen. It is now in ruins. But the painted pictures on its walls are among the finest in Nubia. Thutmose the Third also erected many monuments in Nubia. He erected a statue at Kalabsha in Lower Nubia, and he also built many temples.

King Ramses the Second liked building temples and erecting statues. Besides the two splendid temples at Abu Simbel, he built many other temples. He built temples in Lower and Upper Nubia. One of these temples is cut in the side of the hill at Beit-el-Wali.

The temple contains an open space, a hall and a sanctuary. A sanctuary is the most sacred place in a temple. Pictures have been cut in the stone walls of the temple. One scene represents an attack on the enemy. Ramses is shown in his chariot. He is followed by princes. Enemy soldiers are seen running to their camp. A wounded soldier is being led away by two of his companions.

In another scene the King is sitting on his throne. A beautiful umbrella is over his head. He is receiving various kinds of presents. He is being given gold rings, ivory furniture, animal-skins, bows, myrrh, oxen, ostrich-eggs and ostrich-feathers. But the most wonderful present is a splendid table. The table is hung with skins and ornamented with flowers.

Nubia was now a very important land for the Egyptians. It supplied the Egyptian army with soldiers. It supplied Egypt with cattle and various kinds of articles. Above all, it supplied her with gold.

* * *

For thousands of years the Ancient Egyptian temples and statues in Nubia remained. They lived to tell the story of Egypt in Nubia. Then a great change came. It has had a serious effect on the monuments. The Nubians themselves have not escaped the effect of the change. But what has caused it?

For a very long time the Egyptians have depended on the Nile for cultivation. Each summer the water rose in the river. It flowed over its banks and covered the fields. Then it gradually went down and the fields were cultivated.

Sometimes a very high flood came and caused much damage. The water of the flood destroyed crops and drowned sheep and cattle. Sometimes whole villages were drowned. At the same time, much of the water of the high flood went into the sea. It could not be kept and used by the people.

But if a high flood was dangerous, a low flood was no less dangerous. During a low flood there was not enough water for the fields. Farmers could not therefore grow their crops. As a result of this, people suffered.

So it was decided that much of the water of the Nile should be saved. It should be saved for times of need. If a dam were built across the river, water could be stored behind it. In 1902 a dam was built at Aswan. It became very useful. But as the population of Egypt grew, more water was needed. The larger the number of people, the greater was the need for water. The water stored behind the Aswan Dam was not enough. Nor could this dam prevent high floods.

So it was decided to build a larger dam. A larger dam could certainly store more water. This was the purpose of the High Dam which is south of Aswan.

The High Dam is a great artificial wall. Unlike the Aswan Dam it is a solid wall. There are no openings in it. But how could the water continue to flow along the river?

A canal was dug in the rock. Six immense tunnels were also dug. A tunnel is a passage under the ground. The water of the river could therefore flow through the canal and the tunnels. The tunnels have large steel gates which are opened and shut to control the flow of water. The water rushing through the tunnels was used to produce electricity. A power-station was built. The station now supplies Egyptian towns and villages with electricity.

The building of the High Dam caused water to rise behind it. The water formed a great reservoir or lake. This is Lake Nasser. Lake Nasser is one of the largest artificial lakes ever made by man. It stretches for three hundred miles south of the High Dam; its average width is six miles.

*　*　*

The High Dam

For thousands of years the Nubians lived in the narrow valley of the Nile. The desert came almost to the banks of the river. There were only narrow strips of land which they could cultivate. Then the High Dam was built and the water rose in Lake Nasser. The fields and the houses of the Nubians were in danger. So were their sheep, cattle and palm-trees. It was therefore decided to move the people to a new land. The new land is far away from the water of the great lake.

The Nubians have now settled in their new land. They are happy in their new homes. But they can hardly forget their old homes and their old villages. They still love them. They love them so much that they have given their new villages old names. The old names of their drowned villages are still very dear to their hearts.

But what happened to the ancient monuments of Nubia? Did they suffer the same fate as the Nubian homes and the Nubian villages?

Chapter 4
The Great Temple of Abu Simbel

One hundred and seventy-four miles south of Aswan stand the two temples of Abu Simbel. Of all the ancient monuments in Nubia, these temples are the most wonderful. It was King Ramses the Great who built these two splendid temples. But the temples were not actually built. They were cut in the mountain. The only part that was built was a terrace. This was built in front of the great temple.

At the time of King Ramses, the Nile came up to the base of the terrace. But the small temple was four metres lower than the great temple. So the water of the river almost touched its door. This happened during the flood. During the rest of the year the river fell gradually. It left a large, level piece of land. This land was cultivated and covered with crops.

The two temples were discovered at the beginning of the nineteenth century. Before that time, heaps of sand

The façade of the Great Temple of Abu Simbel

had hidden them from view. Then in 1813 a traveller called Ludwig saw large stone faces. They seemed to be coming out of the sand. He knew that the stone faces belonged to large statues. But were they sitting or standing statues? The traveller could not find out. In 1817 the sand was taken away. The statues and the temples appeared.

But why did King Ramses choose that part of Nubia for such splendid temples? Was it because the land there was so beautiful and so solemn? Or because the Ancient Egyptians believed that the hills beyond the river were sacred? Or did the great Pharaoh want to show the people of the south his power and wealth? Perhaps all these reasons influenced his choice.

Four great statues ornament the façade of the great temple. They seem to guard the front part of the temple. The immense size of these statues is really astonishing. Each is about twenty metres high. The statues represent King Ramses the Second. He is wearing the double crown of Egypt and sitting on a large throne. Pictures cover the sides of the throne. The pictures represent the union between the two lands of Egypt: Upper and Lower Egypt. Two gods of the Nile are binding flowers: the lotus and the papyrus, which represent the two parts of the country.

The thrones are placed on high bases. Each base looks like a big box. The eldest son of Ramses the Second is seen on the front part of each base. He is dressed like a priest and is showing respect to the King's names. Pictures of prisoners of war cover the sides of the bases.

Besides the four great statues, there are smaller statues. The smaller statues represent the members of the royal family. Some are standing on each side of the King. Others are between his legs. Some of these statues are of immense size. But, compared with the four great statues,

The feet of one of the statues of the Great Temple

they look very small. The four great statues of the King can only be compared to the mountain itself.

The temple has a narrow door. It is in the centre of the façade and in the middle of the four great statues. Above the door of the temple, a statue is cut out of the rock. It stands in a hollow place in the façade. It is the statue of the god Ra-Horakhty, who was the god of the rising sun. Here he is the chief god of the temple. He is represented with a human body and the head of a wild bird. On his head, he is carrying the disc of the sun. A disc is a small circle. A royal stick with the head of a wild animal is on his right. The figure of the goddess Maet is on his left. Maet was the goddess of justice and truth. The royal stick, the goddess Maet and the sun-disc together make the name: *User-Maet-Ra*. This is the name of the sun-god. It is also one of the names of King Ramses.

Pictures of the King appear on each side of the statue. They are cut in the façade. The King is seen making an offering. He is offering the figure of Maet to the god Ra-Horakhty.

The whole temple was built in honour of King Ramses and the god Ra-Horakhty. The King wanted to be united with the gods. The four great statues, in front of the temple, do not show him as a human creature. Instead they represent him as a god.

Higher up, at the top of the façade, there is a row of baboons. The Ancient Egyptians believed that baboons were sacred animals. The baboons are sitting on their back paws. They are raising their front paws and welcoming the rising sun.

The door of the temple leads to a great hall. Two rows of pillars seem to support the roof of the hall. There are four pillars in each row. Each pillar is about eight metres high. The pillars divide the hall into three passages. The middle passage is twice as wide as the side passages.

Against the pillars stand eight big statues. Their faces are turned towards the middle passage. The statues represent King Ramses, who is shown here as the god Osiris. By the side of his head, hieroglyphic letters are cut in the stone. The letters say, "The good god, lord of the two lands, the one who is loved by Amon." These are some of the titles of King Ramses.

On the three other sides of the pillars, there are religious scenes. The King is making offerings to various gods. On one of the pillars, Bentanta is making an offering to a goddess. Bentanta was the King's wife and she was also his daughter.

The roof of the hall is ornamented with pictures of the vulture. This wild bird is spreading its wings. It is protecting the building and the names of the King.

Pictures which have been cut in the stone ornament the walls of the hall. Pictures on each side of the door show the King killing his enemies. He is doing this before the god Amon, on the south side. On the north side, he is killing his enemies before the god Ra-Horakhty.

Scenes of the battle of Kadesh cover the north wall. The famous battle is described in detail. All the main events of the battle are here shown in beautiful pictures: the Pharaoh's council of war; the King's camp guarded by his soldiers; the arrest and the beating of the two Hittites; and then the fierce battle, and the confused struggle of horses and chariots. Enemy soldiers lie dying. The Hittite leader is shown running away. But one figure controls the whole scene. This is the splendid figure of King Ramses.

Three other scenes of war ornament the south wall of the great hall. The pictures still preserve their bright colours. On the left the King is seen standing in his chariot. He is pulling his bow and aiming an arrow at an enemy fortress. The enemies are unable to resist and are

A picture of the battle of Kadesh

giving themselves up. A man and his cattle are seen running away. They are afraid of the fierce attack of the Pharaoh.

In the next scene, the King is holding a spear in his hand. He is fighting on the ground with an enemy. The unhappy man is pushed back. The King drives his spear into his body. Under the Pharaoh's feet there is another enemy who has been knocked down by the King.

After this, there is the scene of the royal procession. The fight has now ended. The King's enemies have already been defeated. The Pharaoh is then seen coming back home. He is driving his horses. An officer is marching before him; his favourite lion is at his side. Two rows of prisoners are being driven in the King's procession. The unhappy men are overcome by despair.

In all the scenes of the great hall, the Ancient Egyptian artist has shown great skill. In beautiful pictures he has described the brave deeds of a great Pharaoh. He has also succeeded in showing human feelings. The faces of the enemy clearly express pain, fear, sorrow and despair.

In the west wall of this hall there are two openings. The openings lead to two groups of store-rooms. In the north wall two other openings also lead to two store-rooms. These rooms contained the objects of worship used by the priests. Many scenes ornament the walls of the store-rooms. The King is seen making offerings. He is either standing or on his knees.

The great hall leads to a smaller hall. Four square pillars seem to support the roof of this hall. Religious scenes ornament the walls and the pillars of the hall. On the pillars, the King is seen with the gods. They welcome him and hold him in their arms.

On the walls, the King is seen with Queen Nefertari. The Queen is playing the sistrum. The King is burning incense before the sacred boat, which is being carried on the shoulders of priests. The Ancient Egyptians believed that the boat carried the gods to the underworld. They also believed that the sacred boat would carry the King to the underworld.

Beyond this hall there is a little room. It is much smaller than the hall of pillars. The walls of the room are covered with beautiful pictures. Once more the King is seen making offerings to the gods.

The little room leads to the sanctuary. Pictures of the sacred boat ornament two walls of the sanctuary. On the south wall, the King is seen burning incense. He is standing before the sacred boat of Amon. On the north wall, he burns incense before the sacred boat of Ra-Horakhty.

In the west wall of the sanctuary, four sitting statues are cut in the rock. These are the gods of the temple: Ptah, Amon, Ramses himself and Ra-Horakhty. Unfortunately these sacred statues bear the marks of much damage. Their beautiful colours have almost disappeared.

In the centre of the sanctuary there is a small stone altar. An altar is a special table used in a temple. It was here that the sacred boat was placed. But the boat is no longer there. It was made of wood, and it therefore decayed.

The sanctuary is also the scene of the "wonder of the sun". The light of the sun enters the sanctuary twice a year: on the twentieth of February and on the twentieth of October. A lady who was visiting the temple noticed this wonder of the sun in 1874. She said, "In the east, the sun comes up above the tops of the hills. Its light enters the temple, and like an arrow it strikes the darkness inside. Then it reaches the sanctuary and at last it falls on the altar. It looks like fire from heaven. It lights the altar and it also lights the four statues." To the modern visitor this is a wonderful experience. So must it have been for the people who worshipped there in ancient times.

Another visitor to the great temple said, "Here one feels how solemn the place is. Indeed, at no other place does one understand so well the Ancient Egyptian spirit of worship."

Chapter 5
The Small Temple

At a short distance to the north of the great temple stands the small temple. It is much smaller than the great temple, but it is one of the finest monuments in Nubia. King Ramses the Second built this temple for his wife, Queen Nefertari. She was a beautiful woman and the King loved her very much. So he built for her this splendid temple.

The temple was also built in honour of the goddess Hathor. Hathor was the goddess of music, dancing and love. The Ancient Egyptians imagined that Hathor had a human body. But she had the horns and ears of a cow. She also carried the disc of the sun on her head.

Six immense statues ornament the façade of the temple. In the centre of the façade is the door of the temple. On each side of the door stand three statues. Each statue is ten metres high. Two statues represent the King and one represents the Queen. In both groups the Queen has

The façade of the Small Temple

the King on each side of her.

The six statues are cut in the rock. They seem to be stepping out of the mountain. Large hieroglyphic letters cover the parts of the rock between the statues. The letters are cut in the stone.

In one part the letters say, "King Ramses the Second has built this temple in the mountain. Such work has never been attempted before." In another part the letters say, "This temple has been built for the great royal wife, Nefertari. It is for her sake that the sun rises."

The Queen is represented as the goddess Hathor. She is carrying on her head the sun-disc with two feathers. She is also holding the sistrum in her hand. On the Queen's left side, to the south, the King is wearing the white crown. On her right, he is wearing the double crown. To the north, he is again wearing the double crown, on the Queen's right. On her left, he is seen with the crown of the god Osiris.

Besides the six immense statues there are smaller statues, which represent the royal children. The princesses are placed on both sides of the Queen. The princes stand on both sides of the King.

A passage leads from the door of the temple to the main hall. The walls of the passage are ornamented with two scenes of offering. On the south side, King Ramses is making an offering to the goddess Hathor. On the north side, Queen Nefertari is making offerings to the goddess Isis.

In the hall one finds oneself in a place full of beauty and charm. In most of the scenes the King and the Queen are shown with flowers in their hands. They are young and beautiful. Indeed, they rival the beauty of the flowers which they are holding.

Six square pillars seem to support the roof of the hall. The front part of each pillar is ornamented with the head of the goddess Hathor. The sides of the pillars are covered with pictures. The pictures represent the goddess Hathor, the goddess Maet and Queen Nefertari. The Queen is holding the sistrum and papyrus flowers.

Pictures on the walls of the hall show a variety of scenes. On both sides of the east wall, the King is seen defeating his enemies. He is doing this before the god Amon, on the south side; and before the god Ra-Horakhty, on the north side. The Queen is seen with the King. She seems to be asking him to have pity on the unhappy men.

On the south wall, Queen Nefertari is seen receiving a necklace from the goddess Hathor. The King is being given a crown by the god Set and the god Anubis, who was the god of embalming. Next the Queen appears before a beautiful goddess. The Queen is offering flowers to her. Then the King is seen again. He is offering the figure of the goddess Maet to the god Amon.

On the opposite wall, the King is seen making an offering to the god Ptah, who was the god of Memphis. He was also the god of art and artists. Then the Queen appears before the goddess Hathor. The Queen is offering flowers to her.

The hall of pillars leads to a little room. Beautiful scenes ornament the east wall of this room. Indeed, the most beautiful picture in the whole temple covers a part of this wall. The little room is very narrow. It allows us just enough space to admire this wonderful picture. The Queen appears between the goddess Hathor and the goddess Isis. The two goddesses are putting a crown on her head. The crown is made up of the sun-disc and the horns of a cow. Two feathers enclose the sun-disc. Nefertari is also receiving the blessings of the goddesses. She has already been raised to the rank of a goddess.

On the other part of the wall, the King is offering

Two goddesses are giving a crown to Queen Nefertari.

flowers to the goddess of child-birth. Queen Nefertari is standing behind him with flowers in her hands.

The south and north walls of the room are also covered with pictures of the King and the Queen. They are seen worshipping the goddess Hathor, who is in her boat.

The King is again seen on the west wall. To the south, he is seen making offerings to the god Amon. To the north, he is making an offering to the god Ra-Horakhty.

The little room leads to the sanctuary. To the right, Ramses is seen worshipping his own figure and that of the Queen. To the left, the Queen is seen worshipping the goddess Hathor and the goddess Mut, who was the goddess of the sky.

In a hollow place in the west wall, a statue of Hathor seems to spring from the rock. Hathor is shown here in the form of a cow. Beneath its head stands the figure of King Ramses, who is claiming the protection of the goddess.

* * *

Our visit to the two old temples has now finished. One can only wonder at the strange beliefs of the Ancient Egyptians which made them put up such splendid monuments. Perhaps no other people in the whole world have left monuments of such immense size. Imagine a modern building made up of six flats, one on top of the other. The big statues in front of the great temple are as high as this building.

How long did it take the Ancient Egyptians to cut out the four great statues in stone? How long did it take them to dig the two temples out of the solid rock? The great temple goes about fifty-five metres deep into the mountain. The Ancient Egyptians did not have our modern machines. Nor did they possess any of our mechanical tools. But with very simple tools they managed to make such splendid monuments.

With very simple tools their artists cut out the beautiful pictures in both temples. The wonder of the sun, since it was discovered, has also astonished the modern visitor.

How could a people who lived in the distant past do all this? What sort of people were they? They must have possessed skill, patience and great wisdom. But did they possess any mysterious power which is still unknown to us?

And what will happen now to their wonderful monuments, the monuments which have long astonished the world? Do not such monuments deserve all our care and protection?

Chapter 6
Save Abu Simbel!

The rising water in Lake Nasser threatened the ancient monuments in Nubia. It threatened the two temples of Abu Simbel. "If the water continues to rise," thought the people, "the temples will soon be drowned." The temples have lived for thousands of years. They tell the story of a great Pharaoh. It would therefore be a great pity if the temples disappeared.

On 9 January 1960, men started to build the High Dam. In 1964 good progress had already been made. Across the great river the immense wall of the dam was rising gradually. The higher the dam rose, the higher the water rose in the lake. And the higher the water rose, the more serious the situation at Abu Simbel became. If no action were taken, the rising water would drown the temples. The world would lose two great treasures. What could be done to save the two wonderful temples?

Egypt approached the United Nations Organization.

Save Abu Simbel!

The United Nations Organization urged its members to help to save the temples. A number of nations were ready to help and actually offered assistance.

But how could the temples be rescued? They were cut deep into the rock. And there was the whole mountain over them. Indeed, rescuing the temples looked very difficult. But man has always managed to overcome the difficulties he meets.

Many plans for rescuing the temples were made. One plan was that the temples should be saved by lifting them up. A part of the mountain hanging over the temples would be taken away. A strong concrete base would be built under each temple. Concrete is a strong building material. The two temples would be enclosed in two immense concrete boxes. Then the boxes enclosing the temples would be raised to a safe place.

But how could such heavy loads be raised? A great number of mechanical jacks would be placed beneath the boxes. The jacks were machines which would raise the temples. They would raise them gradually, a millimetre at a time. When the jacks were fully stretched, concrete pillars would be placed under the boxes. This would be repeated until the temples were high enough.

But this bold plan was not accepted since it would cost a lot of money. Another plan was that a permanent dam should be built round the temples. This plan was not accepted either. In spite of the dam, water would get through and damage the temples. So, to keep them dry, machines would be necessary in order to pump out the water. This would also cost a lot of money. There was also another problem. The dam would prevent the light of the sun from entering the great temple. This would rob the temple of the wonder of the sun. It would rob it of its real secret.

At last it was decided to carry out an entirely different

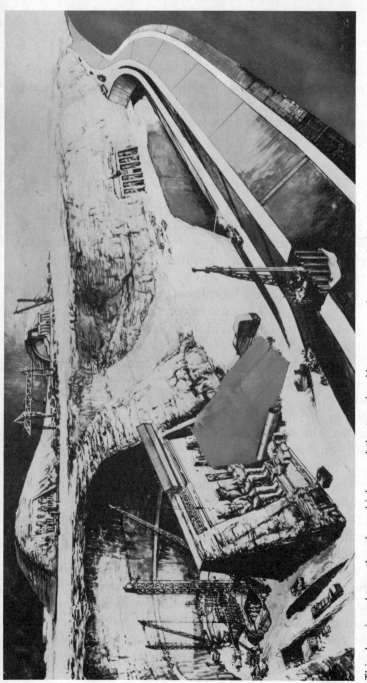

This drawing shows the plan which saved the temples. You can see the water behind the protecting dam; the old position of the temples; the piles of sand in front of two statues; the steel tunnel into the temple; and, at the top of the picture, the new position of the temples.

plan. The two temples would be cut into large pieces. The pieces would be put together again. But they would be put together in a higher position; and farther from the river. In this way they would be safe. This plan also had the lowest cost.

* * *

The work of rescuing the temples was carried out by a group of companies. The companies belonged to different nations. There were engineers, architects, archaeologists and workmen from different nations. An archaeologist studies ancient monuments.

At present the two temples of Abu Simbel stand high on the mountain. They are beyond the water of the great artificial lake. The Pharaoh looks proud and happy. Sitting on his throne he seems pleased at the work which has been done. His wounds have healed. He seems to smile down upon the great river. The river looks far wider than it was in ancient times. For centuries the light of the sun has entered the great temple and has reached the sanctuary. It does so now. But how has all this been done?

At first the archaeologists did not like the idea of cutting the temples into pieces. They thought that the temples might be destroyed in this way. But the water in the river was rising. So it was a race against time. And cutting the temples was the quickest way. Indeed, the temples were rescued just in time.

Work started at Abu Simbel in the spring of 1964. The building of the High Dam had already started. For the first time the Nile was flowing in its new bed. The main river had already been blocked by the dam. The water started to rise. The engineers at Abu Simbel did not have much time. The water would soon rise to one hundred and thirty-two metres above sea level. The base of the small temple was one hundred and twenty metres above sea level. The base of the great temple was four metres higher.

Therefore, to rescue the temples, it was necessary to build a dam. The dam would protect the temples against the rising water. It would not be a permanent dam, but it would last only until the work of cutting the temples was complete. But if work at Abu Simbel had started earlier, the dam would not have been necessary.

To put up this dam, sheets of steel were used. The sheets had to be driven deep enough to reach solid ground. They were driven eleven metres deep. Heaps of rocks and sand supported the sheets of steel on both sides.

To complete the dam in time, the engineers and workmen worked hard. They were not worried about their own comfort. They were in a hurry. But in spite of this, they had anxious moments. In November 1964, the water in the river rose. It was only two metres from the top of the dam. The engineers were worried. The higher the water rose, the more worried they became.

But this dangerous situation did not last for long. The engineers managed to win the battle against the rising water. In the spring of 1965, the dam was complete. It started south of the great temple, and stretched as far as the cliff which is to the north of the small temple. Water was prevented from reaching the temples. This was a great success. The temples were no longer in danger.

But small quantities of water still went through. This was annoying. For the place in front of the temples had to be kept dry. Immediate action was therefore taken. Narrow canals were dug. These canals collected the water which came through the dam.

Deep wells were also dug and these caused the level of water on the ground to fall. They also supplied the people at Abu Simbel with drinking-water. Sometimes pumps were used, to take away the water and to keep the place dry.

* * *

Certainly King Ramses never dreamed of the busy scene in front of his great temple. Pumps, machines, tools and building materials filled the place. But if he came back to life, he would be pleased. Preparations had already been made for the rescue of his temples.

But how could such a large number of engineers and workmen live in the desert? At the busiest time there were about two thousand people living at Abu Simbel. What kind of life did they have?

At first they erected their tents and huts on the bank of the river. But the water of the Nile rose. So they moved farther from the bank, to higher ground. Houses were built and roads were made. A small town was formed. There were shops, offices, a club, a cinema and a swimming-pool. There were also a hospital, a power-station and a small harbour. Gardens surrounded the houses, and birds sang in the trees. Indeed, in the heart of the desert, the place looked like a beautiful oasis.

But how could the people of this beautiful oasis get what they needed? They could not get any supplies from the Nubian villages. There was nobody there. The people had already left in order to go to their new homes in the north.

So the only place to get supplies from was Aswan, one hundred and seventy-four miles to the north. Boats were used. One boat was called *Ramses the Second.* Another was called *Nefertari.* Three small aeroplanes were also used, to carry people and mail across the desert. They also carried light articles which were urgently needed.

But carrying supplies from Aswan to Abu Simbel was not the only problem. Many supplies had to be brought from abroad. Much of the heavy material came from other countries. So a system was planned. Supplies came from Europe to Alexandria by sea. Then they were carried to Aswan by boat and by car.

As work continued, the people at Abu Simbel began to know each other better. They came from different countries and spoke different languages. But this did not prevent them from becoming good friends. Indeed, it was a happy international organization at Abu Simbel. The people worked together and helped each other. And the more progress was made, the more friendly they became. All of them had one wish. They wished to defeat the rising water and to rescue the two wonderful treasures.

Chapter 7
The Rescue of the Pharaoh

To cut the two temples into pieces, the roofs of both had to be reached. To reach the roofs, the top of the mountain had to be taken away. This was not easy. It needed a lot of work. Besides, pieces of stone might fall from the mountain. They might fall on the statues, which were three thousand two hundred years old, and damage them. Falling stones might also damage the sacred baboons. A wooden frame was therefore put over the baboons. But how could the great statues be protected?

It was decided to cover them with sand. This could hardly be done by hand, since a very large space had to be filled. Machines were therefore used. Bulldozers pushed piles of sand up to the chests of the sitting statues. A bulldozer is a large machine which is used for moving heavy objects. Other machines poured sand over their heads and crowns. The space in front of the great temple was soon filled up with sand. The great statues of Ramses the Second disappeared. They now lay buried under a great pile of sand. Indeed, the place reminded people of a scene in the past. It reminded them of the time when the temples were discovered.

But how could the inside of the temple be reached? Would not the sand block the doorway? To keep the doorway open, a steel tunnel was made. Before the façade was covered with sand, the tunnel had been placed in position. Another steel tunnel was made for the small temple. The façade of the small temple had also been covered with sand.

The four great statues were now safe. So were the statues in front of the small temple. But the roofs and walls of the temples were not safe. They were in danger. Cutting rocks above the temples might damage them and the roofs might even fall down. So steel bars were put up inside the temples. They supported the roofs and protected the walls. They also helped the workmen to reach the roofs.

To join the bars together, electric machines were used. Showers of sparks fell over the statues in the great temple. This was very interesting. King Ramses the Great was covered with a shower of sparks. Perhaps the Ancient Egyptian artist had never dreamed of such an amusing scene.

Outside the temples, much was being done. Workmen had already started to cut rocks from the mountain. At the same time, plans were being discussed for the next action. The two temples would be cut into blocks and the blocks would be taken away. The engineers were discussing these problems.

The engineers also considered the tools that should be used. The temples were made of sandstone. Sandstone is a very delicate stone. Careful treatment of the stone was therefore necessary.

A head is being lifted from the sand.

The Rescue of the Pharaoh

To cut the stones, it was decided to use two kinds of saw. The motor-saw would be used for the back parts of the temples. But for cutting the blocks at the front, it was decided to use a hand-saw.

The cuts in the stones had to be very narrow. They should not be wider than six millimetres. Cuts in the richly ornamented stones should be even narrower. It was very important to preserve these precious monuments in their original condition.

Raising the cut stones was another problem. The blocks were heavy. Most of them weighed twenty tons each and some weighed even more. How could these blocks be lifted without being damaged? Deep holes were made in each block. Then steel bars were driven deep into the holes.

To fix the bars firmly into the holes, a special substance was used. This substance was chosen after many tests had been made. Then, to lift the blocks, mechanical cranes were used. A crane is a tall machine which is used to lift heavy objects.

But before lifting the cut parts, all the rocks above the temples had to be taken away. Bulldozers were used. They broke the rock and carried the broken rocks away. Work went on for several months. Then, when the roofs were near enough, the bulldozers stopped. Workmen used mechanical hammers which they held in their hands. They continued to work until they reached the roofs. The roofs were now almost one metre thick.

Men working inside the temples could hear the sound of the hammers outside. Conditions were not always comfortable for these men. Cutting the rock caused much dust to come out. The dust filled the halls and rooms of the temples. Men had to wear masks to protect their eyes and lungs from the harmful dust.

But dust was not the only problem. Sometimes the

men could not stand upright on the steel bars. They had to bend their bodies very low, in a very painful position. But although they suffered much, they did not complain. Their only interest was in the cuts they were making. They tried to make the cuts as narrow as possible. When they succeeded they were very satisfied.

At last the time came for lifting the first block. A large and heavy block was made loose. The day was very hot, but the heat did not prevent the workmen from hurrying to the scene. They stopped work and gathered in front of the great temple. The engineers were also there. All eyes were fixed on the block. It was an anxious moment.

There were very anxious moments when the important blocks were carried away. The face of the Pharaoh, the standing statues in the great hall, the stones showing the battle of Kadesh or the crowning of Nefertari: all these were important blocks. But this block was an ordinary one. Yet much depended on the success of lifting it and carrying it away. This would prove the success of all the plans for rescuing the temples.

Slowly the big block was raised by the long arm of the crane. For a moment the heavy load seemed to hang in the air. Then it was slowly and carefully let down. It was let down onto a big trailer filled with sand. The sand in the trailer made a soft pillow for the big stone. The trailer was moved very slowly because any shaking might have damaged the block.

The first block was followed by other blocks. When the roofs of the two temples were gone, daylight came in. For the first time since the building of the temples, light filled the halls and rooms inside.

It was then the turn of the great statues. The sand which had covered them had already been taken away. Workmen started cutting the statues into blocks. They had to be very careful. Care was also taken when the blocks were being lifted. Indeed, it was an exciting moment when the first face of the statues was lifted. The block was very precious. The four great statues were cut in the rock more than three thousand years ago. Now, after such a long time, they were going to be moved.

The two temples were cut into one thousand and forty-two blocks. Each block was marked with letters and figures. These showed the original position of the blocks in the temples. The blocks would be put together again. The figures and letters would help the workmen to put each block into its proper place.

The first part of the work now came to an end. The temples had been cut into blocks which were lifted and carried away safely. Not a single block was broken. Not a single block was even cracked. This was a great victory for all the people who had been given this important work. On 31 March 1966, they received a telegram from the United Nations Organization which congratulated them on their success. They truly deserved to be congratulated.

* * *

The dam which had protected the two temples was no longer needed. The water of the great river was therefore allowed to come in. It filled the whole place. In place of the two old temples there were now two great caves filled with water.

But where did the blocks of the two temples go? They were taken to a high place in the desert. The place had already been prepared for storing the blocks. The ground had been made level. But there was nothing to protect the blocks. Linen strips had already been carefully put round the ornamented blocks, but this was not enough. All the stones had to be covered with mats

The head of Ramses II is lifted to its new position.

King Ramses

The last pieces of a statue are being taken away.

which protected them against the heat of the sun. They also protected them from the sandstorms which often blow in the desert.

The parts of the two temples now lay scattered on the ground. For centuries the four great statues had been standing proudly in front of the great temple. Now they lay in pieces on the sand of the desert. Nor was the fate of the sacred baboons much better. For thousands of years they had welcomed the rising sun every morning. They had been placed high above the door of the great temple. Now they too lay on the ground.

Certainly the archaeologists were not pleased. The two splendid temples were reduced to pieces of stone lying on the ground. Without doubt the archaeologists were eager to see the temples rebuilt. Indeed, the sooner they were put up again the better. But the engineers and the architects did everything according to plan. Every action was considered before any decision was taken.

In January 1966, work started on the rebuilding of the temples. A little ceremony was held, to show the importance of the occasion. Many people attended the ceremony. Some represented the Egyptian Government. Others were sent by the United Nations Organization.

The crane was again used to let down the blocks of stone. Each block was carefully placed in its proper position. The steel bars were again put up to support the walls and the roofs. The cuts which had been made in the stones were filled up.

By the end of the year the work of rebuilding the two temples was complete. They now lay beyond the water of the lake. But this was not the end of the affair. The land surrounding the temples had to be changed. The mountain above the temples had to look as it had done in ancient times. So an artificial mountain had to be put up. Great quantities of rock would be placed over

The statues are in their new position. You can see the places where they were cut.

the temples. Concrete had been used to support the walls and the roofs of the temples. But the walls and the roofs were not strong enough to carry the weight of a mountain.

This was a difficult problem for the engineers. But they had already dealt with many difficult problems. This one would not therefore be too difficult for them to overcome. They planned to put up concrete domes over the temples. The domes would protect the temples from the heavy weight above them.

The engineers made plans for putting up the two domes. They had many complicated problems. To solve these problems they used electronic computers. The electronic computers helped them to make correct decisions. Without the computers it would have taken a long time to solve these problems.

The domes were so strong that they could support very heavy weights. They could carry thousands of tons. No domes had ever been built before to support such great weights.

How strong would the domes over the temples be in the future? Would they be able to bear such heavy weights? The engineers felt confident. They were sure that their plans were correct. But it was necessary to keep watch. The effect of weight on the domes must be carefully observed.

After a year and a half, the domes and the artificial mountain had been built. It was now the middle of 1968. The work which had started in May 1964 was now complete. The engineers and the workmen were proud of what they had done. So was all the world. The wonderful temples of Abu Simbel had been preserved. Two treasures dear to the whole world had been rescued.

* * *

The temples stand in their new position. The water of the Nile is beginning to cover their old position.

Visitors to Abu Simbel can now go there either by air or by boat. They can fly from Aswan to Abu Simbel. But if they prefer to go by boat, they may take the hydrofoil. The hydrofoil can reach Abu Simbel in about five hours. It travels at a very great speed and almost flies over the surface of the water. At Abu Simbel visitors can see the two ancient temples. They can see the wonderful treasures which have been so successfully rescued.

* * *

If Ramses the Great came back to life, he would be very grateful to the modern engineer. Without the efforts and the skill of the modern engineer, the temples would have been drowned. The water of the Nile would have become their tomb.

But now the god-like statues can look proudly on the great river. In their new and high position they are quite safe. Once more the sacred baboons can welcome the morning sun. Once more the light of the sun can reach the sanctuary of the great temple. The wonder of the sun, which happens twice a year, shows the skill of the ancient architect. And without the skill of the modern engineer, this wonder would have disappeared.

The temples have been saved. They stand in the light of the sun.